Jack
and
Rusty

by Aleesah Darlison

illustrated by Maxime Lebrun

OXFORD
UNIVERSITY PRESS
AUSTRALIA & NEW ZEALAND

Jack and Rusty were best friends.
They played with the dog.

They raced . . .

... and they **roared!**

3

On the weekend, Jack and Rusty
drew dinosaurs.

"Jack, did you make this mess?"
said Dad.

"It was Rusty!" said Jack.

But it was not Rusty. It was Jack!
So Rusty ran away.

Jack looked and looked for his friend.

But Rusty was not there.

"Jack, did you put snails in here?" said Dad.

"Yes," said Jack. "It was me."

Jack did not play with the dog or race or roar.

"Oh, Rusty," said Jack. "I am sorry!
I miss you. Please come home."

Rusty looked down at Jack.

That night, Rusty got into bed next to Jack.

Jack had his best friend back.

Retell the Story